Just

North

Of

Malibu

A poetry collection by Jolynn Freed Regan

cover design credit: Carla Marlenée Bates

for Simba, Spencer, Sophie & Shandy

CONTENTS

Los Angeles

Hope Street

Generous Enthusiasm

While I Walked

Flower Shower

Griffith Observatory

Kobe

Roger That!

Girls, Girls, Girls

21-Gun Silence

Hold Please

Pledge of Abortion

Awaits

Inside Voice

Black and Blue

Today the Music Died

Tilly

Malibu

My Latitude and Longitude

Sleeping giants gingerly hold morning alive,
their roots spread anticipation with a fervor where I wake.
Always New York, St. James Church, my omen,
staggering snowfall, my blizzard of tears.
At any moment, Barbarians could storm the gates.

Now Malibu, barefoot in the driving rain,
wind wept wildly in Santa Ana rage.
Closed PCH slid hills into arid streets, dredging ideas into ink.

Again New York, Caffe Reggio, a cappuccino in search of self,
where Café Wha? heard Bob Dylan launching.
My bags packed with liberation,
My latitude and longitude.

Broad Beach

Sun peeks from the horizon, risin'
arms stretch wide, waking wonder
midweek, taste of white peaches still sweet on my tongue
soothing salt water licks my toes
sand fills in-between
tickling giggles
negative ions nestle in my mind
sandy feet on this seaside Ferris wheel
starfish and sea stars stand at attention
translucent shells shine, heart-shaped rocks did I mention
seaweed and air duel it out for effervescence
roller coaster waves, dolphins whirl
seahorse riders race offshore
this low-tide, zephyr light-fantastic coastal carnival
bend down, stand-up, run, cartwheel, fly
I ride free
and merry, I go round

Fusing

The fork in the road
polished, shiny, silver or gold
Choices, chances
unfold.
Skipping down the path less picked
Lit by moon and stars in stride,
Jasmine dreams smell sticky sweet
Where no two roads collide.
Or trudging down the dusty dank
en mass with heathen hordes,
whatever golden disillusion says
life misspent, gorged.
I do not flip that copper coin
Letting the odds decide,
Risking road rage, guts strewn about
Scoring raw, bloody hide.
I am well on my path of ruby rose glee
handpicked and plucked,
Exploring the epic underscore
Fusing endurance with some luck.

The Fire Circle

We cross the classroom threshold, to behold, students on the brink of creation; transforming to unleash youths' wisdom words.

We whisper stories, beginnings of poetry, Chumash surrounding the fire circle,

chanting melodies, telling tall tales under cotton candy heaven, melting citrine setting sun

pounding ocean in pastel paradise, Malibu.

CRASH CRASH

Inside their fire circle now, adolescent cries crack the paint.

Love Hate School Shootings

Words sting, then sing. Burning embers shooting sparks into their moon within.

THUD THUD

The Woolsey Fire The Pandemic Assault
Racism

They collapse then explode through lessons; feelings dripping off the page.

CRACK CRACK

The Franklin Fire Alcoholism Suicide
Abortion

Beating in their hearts breaking open, they bleed truth.

THUMP THUMP

The Fire Circle cont.

Sexism The Palisades Fire The Eaton Fire
Addiction

Their ink fuels the flames only they can light,

illuminating darkness dancing round and round.

HOWL HOWL

Adolescent alchemy always up for grabs.

Catch their words in the fire circle.

Just North of Malibu

Five lights in the sky shoot razor-thin arrows into the Pacific

six miles north off the coast

in Point Dume

The Trench

an underwater alien base

thousands of sightings by surfers, scuba divers, sunset chasers

same place, same recollections

zero proof

holy grail of the UFO

infamous, empirical, enormous tranche of an anomaly,

submerged mystifying murk

meticulously constructed, gravity-defying sub-stacked alien condos

above precisely-perfect sunken UFO parking spaces

The Trench

an underwater alien base

massive amounts of conflicting intelligence

about artificial intelligence stokes the

untethered, unhinged, unsolved, eternal mystery,

just North of Malibu

The Catalina

She rocks and rolls
on a sparkling sapphire tapestry
between shores of sand
offering joy
freedom
revealing the lofty lore
of a ship on sea
hearts aboard
in love and life
lifting her sails
to the shifting sky
always smiling, waving goodbye

Astronomical Twilight on Trancas

coasting down Pacific Coast Highway, winding towards home
deep dive Malibu, carnelian paint strokes sunset
twilight soiree guests arrive, Trancas Canyon my turn
I roll windows down, witness darkness speed up
hundred-year-old oak tree's shadow looms
hides red tail hawk, *defying*
white barn owl posted on fence wire head full swivel, *spying*
her silky feather edges silence flight sound
racoons run our ravine in their custom-fit night goggles
coyotes bark to kin, ancient Chumash whisper chants
steady winds blend their harmony
beneath Zenith, Pacific Reed, Prairie June,
wild Indian Grass grows, *ocean flows*
weave nautical twilight with misty dew in scattered night
each star a twinkle in celestial debut, my breath on hold,
behold
twirling up Trancas astronomical twilight has hit,
nothing lit
I park in galaxy ignition
outshine Supernova nights bright end.

full moon mama

she sways under the shine
drinking the milky way
translucent shadow basking
          full moon mama

scented in sage
open in the circle
feet singing songs of spirits long ago
          full moon mama

notes aching to be heard
dance, roar, dance, dance
her hymn forever entranced
          full moon mama

Positive Signs

gritty, grey ash now our home

not even the chimney stood

the sign that hung over our front door

mantra of our every day

that thing I said to myself on the way out of my house

sometimes five times a day when the kids were little

Think Positive!

this place was bustling

now dissolved destruction, wrapped in embers irony

my quicksand of sorrow

there it IS

Think Positive!

I lift the sign, fall to my knees

how can this be all that survived, how can this be *here*

fate what will this cost my reason

there it is

Think Positive!

soul cracked, esophagus burning

I choke on the rupture of my resolve

turn, walk to my car, hold this half-baked sign

my trickling breaths of hope

Think Positive!

Red Lady Spark

Enter the juggernaut of creation

Magic wand sparks, sound bowl hums

A woman's soul singing the song of raven red reality

Exhaling the fire, inhaling the revolution of love

Authentic vision forever in her heart

Setting the world aglow with noisy spirits

Sound safari

Sparkling in her far away

Fickle

There is no salvation
In the head
That turns too quickly
With that fickle, hazy gaze
To see what they think
Choose your heart
Within it beats
Drums of a deeper
Authenticity
Permanent permission
To be yourself

Birute

Ravishing eyes twinkling
behind the original rose-colored glasses
cheeks swell smile
lover of
    rebirth
    knitting
    orchids
    the Lord
    under a full moon party
well-curated, charming brilliance
air tonic allure as she floats by
gratitude, kind Birute
your infinite heart open
gifting present love

fear less / brave more

i don't want your lessons
or advice
i am not seeking solace
i want to languish in the
uncomfortability
of it all
the chasm
cavernous dark holes
we climb down
i want to be sticky
in the mud of silence
uncover greys / with yellow
free gallows / with hope
see fear / with less
seek brave / with more

Wildflowers

the fields wide open for dreams to wander

deep in that ground the sweet scent

of promise

growth

opportunity

she planted her wishes with the wildflowers

FREED

This poem is dedicated to Arlis Leola Reidlinger Freed, my Mom…She was divine hope and promise

A blanket of snow
Sparkles atop soils of solitude
miles and miles
as far as the eye can see.
A snaggle of sadness
Snared, suffocates me.
It was those days when the sea
sank sweetly into my heart,
her diamonds winking on her shiny blue top.
She was divine hope and promise
calling me away from arid acres of desolation.
The chill of the cold-mind
coughs me right out of my frozen Fargo
into her ocean of light.
The sea and me,
One soul,
warm,
          Freed.

Los Angeles

HOPE STREET

"Flowers of all hue, and without thorn the rose." *- John Milton*

Hope Street   *about an hour away.*

Hope Street / oftentimes hope less

humanity hovers here

shadows in tents and trash

you should come meet her

Hope Street   *about an hour away.*

Hope Street / she tries you

asking / you don't want to talk

smiling / keep coming back

beautiful / my name for you

Hope Street   *about an hour away.*

Hope Street / a mandala

roses placed on table

peeling petals

today

she spoke / hope full

Hope Street   *about an hour away.*

Generous Enthusiasm

Live each day

with gratitude

and

generous enthusiasm

so as

never to remember

any day

with regret

While I Walked

For the women and girls left in Afghanistan August 30, 2021

If I wanted to
I could go for a walk outside today
with anyone
I wanted to
Wearing anything
I wanted to
And I wanted to
so, I did.
I walked wherever
I wanted to go, wearing whatever
I wanted to wear
or didn't, talking to whomever
I wanted to, saying whatever
I wanted to,
I didn't hesitate, stop to think or tempt fate.
I just spoke and walked and wore
My freedom
Outside
For you today,
While I walked.

FLOWER SHOWER

"Out of all the flowers, me thinks a rose is best." - William Shakespeare

The morning I walked in, saw you sitting at a table,

tiny in the chair, maybe six-years-old

roses in my hand for our meditation, intention to do
something rooted, special to make you feel special

because flowers don't grow here.

"Wanna play a game," I ask?

"Have you ever played flower shower," I exclaim!

"Whaaaaaaaaaaat," you giggle.

"Let me show you," I smile.

You squeeeeeeeel!

This game is full of wishes in petals and petals of wishes

with our wonder and will, with the dozen I brought

peel petal place wish, peel petal place wish, into our basket
they fall, one, two, three, four

silken soft tissues of hope.

You stand in the middle of this musty, dusty-cornered,
dank room as I sing, "Twirl, twirl flower girl!"

whirling around, making me dizzy, your eyes closed, me by
your side dropping petals from above

Flower Shower cont.

falling all over you, around you, beside you, below you

stuck in your hair, on your shoulders, on top of your two-sizes too big slippers

everywhere you smell of sweetness.

Fresh, clean and free in your shower of flowers

gone, rank stink of judgement

I whisper, "Put these in your pocket."

You delicately place petals one by one by one until all your pockets are full

Inhale possibility.

Later that day, I walk out of St. Francis, front door

see you across the street, crouched on the curb hiding under your mom's arm

you notice me, hop up

reach into your right front pocket and gently pull petals

your smile lights Hope Street.

This poem was written over ten years ago

I never saw this little girl or her mother again after that day

I often wonder about her, send her love

I could have been that girl but I was adopted by two loving hearts, placed roses on my table

I hope she thinks of me and forever remembers that day we shared our flower shower.

Griffith Observatory

rose quartz / sacred selenite crystals packed

sage gently wrapped / my meditation mat

anticipation magnified / through Zeiss Mark IV

about 55 minutes East / my top 5 fav LA gemstore

first visit thirty years ago / major axis lines aligned

sublime

perfect N. S. E. W. meridian coincides here /

mother nature cosmos reside here

this prominent planetarium

where angels adjust their wings / international soul's sing

icon of observatory Los Angeles / a gift

from Griffith J. Griffith

whose parents were notorious for their lack of creativity /
dull sense of humor / now I'm bereft

Griffith rather generous of spirit / did not hold a grudge

1919 found him handing the City of LA this terrestrial land
/ now you be the judge

Hollywood directed her spotlight here / in the shadow of
that infamous sign

Rebel Without A Cause drove James Dean to this spot /
bronze sculpture proof of his crime

Griffith Observatory cont.

Arnold Schwarzenegger / opened fire with his Terminator
Transformers cars unfold / box office gold
Charlie's Angels femme fatale' Full Throttle /
those babes were bold
85M people have walked here / for free
tonight / just me
party of one / a mesmerizing mythical date with planet LA
grasp the golden railing with both hands /
I stand on the marble stairway
gaze up at my North Star

Kobe

phenom

Oscar winner

No. 8

alley-oop

elation

tongue dangling

savior

artist

warrior

symbol of LA

accused

Black Mamba

No. 24

infamous fade-away

statue at Staples

crash in Calabasas

this poem unfinished

like

his

life

Roger That!

first day / dream career pinnacle / prestigious LA PR firm

Pacific Coast Highway / seaside paradise / my freeway to work

waves pumpin' / dolphins jumpin'

conquer climb California incline / glide onto world-famous Santa Monica Boulevard

trusty Thomas Guide by my side

glance over to see semi-truck speeding down this iconic street / Neanderthal

mudflaps stamped / Fargo, North Dakota

I *grew up* in Fargo, North Dakota / ironic

right on Century Park East / road rhyme high-rise haiku

my turn / twin towers / two tallest on the block

pull my ticket underground parking / board art deco elevator swing music pipin'

Lobby floor / dry cleaner / car wash / valet / in case you're running late

definitely not in Fargo anymore, a place where *no one* is late

next elevator / solid oak accordion doors / glinting gold carved leaves adorned

push 22nd floor / viola / I have arrived

Roger That! cont.

Rogers & Associates logo / precisely placed above creamy silver etched granite reception desk

this creation should be moved immediately / LA Museum of Contemporary Art

no receptionist / golden LA daylight kisses my face

glance down / new Tag Huer professional watch / 7:20am

I'm early / I breathe

elevator doors open / enter the storied success

dapper in a three-piece suit / grin like Michael Landon

son of Henry C. Rogers / AKA Cary Grant of public relations / the original

Ron Rogers / LA power-broker / Mayor and Police Chief frequent flyers

loves wide-open spaces / his ranch in Colorado

my boss / company owner / legendary namesake / enlightener of ethics

Good morning / *you're here early* / that smile

I follow as he peppers questions / turns on lights

I make sure to note every switch

How ya doin? / How was your drive in today? / What freeway did you take? / Traffic bad?

Roger That! cont.

I'm electrified / walking in a mind-blown haze / waves his arm to welcome me in

This is you / Come by my office around 10am / We'll go over things / Roger That!

he half-laughs / turns the corner / heads down the hall

these walls scented in success / creative consciousness

my office / Queen of England inspired desk / bronze baroque / mother of pearl

I fall into what must be the most ergonomically correct chair I have ever sunken into

too comfy / could doze off

were it not for irony pinching me hard / long on the cheek

as I turn / outside my window / perfect view of the world-famous Hollywood sign

this scene / exact replica of the postcard I kept on my bulletin board in Fargo / for the past 15 years

present / the universe / Hollywood / postcards / PR / me

Ron has since passed / my memories from that morning never will

when I'm in the office early enough / I walk around

turn on all the lights / note the location of every switch

await our newest employee / whisper *Roger That!*

GIRLS GIRLS GIRLS

We forget to tell them they are enough

Enough

we forget to gush too much

simplicity of overflow love

from the woman

for the girls

becoming women

It can be confusing

It will be work

It will be worth it

to wait

for the eventual understanding

that all the roads

lead to your truth

hearts out

smarts exploding

skipping away from convention

on your own path to being

21-Gun Silence

Headline: *19 children and two adults killed, along with 17 injured, at Robb Elementary School.*

Stifling breath struggles in, searing horror on my heart.

I am still here, they are not.

Can we walk into this future?

I'd pray, but I'm tired and silent, I can't.

Let's scream and cry and shout until our throats

are *RED* with the blood spilled.

Will change come to save little hands opened to the heavens?

Bang Bang

Gavels Hit

Like bullets in their bodies.

Ripping at headlines that nothing changes,

when everything did.

Hold Please

Published on the two-year anniversary of the Cali Covid shutdown

How do we know trauma we feel

Without feeling it yet

Stop everything

Hold Please

For years

Hold Please

To the belief that hope will be there

Hold Please

To the memory of touching others

Hold Please

To playing together with strangers

Hold Please

To a mask with a face

The truth of now, unmasked

Hold Please

Infected by this reality

Hold Please

No switch to off

Blinding unprocessed darkness

Green light of hate turned on

Hold Please

The Pledge of Abortion©

I pledge allegiance to my Womb
and the United State of my Body,
and to my Freedom
for which it stands,
one Soul under Me,
indivisible,
with choice of abortion
for all.

Awaits

There is peace in the greyness of not knowing,

sinking with questions in the stillness of an unconscious truth,

that peace isn't calm at all.

It's joy in the corner of your chaos, the eye of story inside your soul.

Enveloped in uncertainty,

yet certain the need to unleash answers.

My peace

Awaits.

Inside Voice

From Minnesota to Gaza children shot, starving, Dead.

This is not a poem I ever want read.

These are not words I want to say,

Poison on my tongue, why would I want them to stay?

School's first day, at Mass, madman shoots two children, Dead.

I cannot stomach now, what unimaginable atrocities ahead?

Would it fix anything if millions unite, together in stride?

Could we get food into Gaza? Guns out of the U.S.? No more kids would, Die?

En masse Mother's march to change what we can, show up, witness, chant, begin.

Reality SMACKS, global challenges too grim.

This is no Mother's sweet storybook read.

If I erase all these words, could there be no more babies, Dead?

Black and Blue

Black and Blue

"What did I do?"

Black and Brown run from reality of being gunned down.

Did nothing wrong

Born Black.

Born Brown.

Rodney looks down remembers well,

no reason those cops beat him to hell.

Brianna home, just lying in bed

no reason to kill

just black, I guess.

The cry for Mama just like George

THAT video, horror, words, hits

bloody murder when

Black and Blue beat together.

How many more, Black and Brown?

How many more, beaten down?

The guns, violence, fists, batons

Why they so angry?

Compassionate humanity, *gone.*

Today The Music Died

For the victims at the Supernova Music Festival on Oct. 7, 2023

Vibrations beating between our ribs,
notes flowing through us.
Musical mystics gyrating, twisting, twirling
in the *free*, open-air.
Powdery pavement under our heels,
kicking up the carousel light-fantastic
spinning all around us.
Pale, rosy sunrise finds us all on the dance floor,
A euphoria of joy,
still.
Until.
"We are coming for you,"
hisses through radios.
Heads turn to horror.
Bodies fall to terror.
Crouch.
          Run.
                    Hide.
Today the music died.

tilly

time tilled in the soil of my life

too little to grow a forest

just enough to plant a seed.

on the horizon, my next poetry chapbook

***Just East In Manhattan* ~ out soon!**

Hotel Chelsea

Stonewalled Inn

Hotel Chelsea

Heavy glass lobby double doors blow me off 23rd street

into this Twilight Zone of ornate rugs ready to be swiped out from under us all

utopian vortex filled with junkie poets, prostitutes, factory girls, playwrights, French models, musicians, speed freaks

strip club on this side of the street, S & M club two doors down

instantaneous freedom and love at first sight

incarnate creators split open spewing grit and glitter

squeezing my painting into your pocket to pay for one more week in her mystical madness

birth of statistics for homo's, addiction, overdoses, suicide, fetish freaks

in shapeless context crisis

abandoned poem drips

my tears alchemize into water for my Nescafe'

one more Kool in the pack

El Quijote holds while we gather

Dylan always at the bar

Hotel Chelsea cont.

Burroughs, Grace, Bob, Janis, Robert and Patti, Jack and
Alan, Salvador and I

no one is anyone yet

fame was never the point

this is

us, here in dialogue blowing artistic altitudes into the wind,
at our usual table

spiritual truths outwit intellect

at the Hotel Chelsea

we change the world

Stonewalled Inn

Steamy summer night in lower Manhattan / my very own jewel box Greenwich Village dream

closet-sized room / sometimes water / always wine

tonight, we dress the occasion / Stonewall in our sights

arrive at 11:11 we giggle / good luck number for us gays

we're queer / we're here / with disregard for favor or living in fear

Stonewall is what we hold dear / freedom

Genovese's own the joint / open season for illegal activities

once a week Officer Dave saunters in / collects gayola / in Hell's Kitchen payola

fat envelopes of cash heavier than Giovanni "GG" Genovese himself

these Inn owners favor hustlers / homeless kids who sleep nearby / us

no liquor license / no running water / no fire exits / still we shimmer wasted every trip

Stonewall's sexual splendor / disrobe judgements weight

upstairs disco glitter beats in my soul / twirl with Marsha and Sylvia like unicorns on magic dust

Stonewalled Inn cont.

our Queen and Queen / two who fight for our right to be queer

early into morning we grind / downing antidotes to hate

undercovers brazen through front doors

second floor safety shatters / commotion stops all motion

Marsha and Sylvia arrested / 6th precinct overflowed

define this generation / with no money for bail

our neighborhood riots / burns / weeps / cracks / bleeds

out to dance with love / four days later still uprising

historical revolution / righteous gay liberation /

53 Christopher Street

ABOUT THE AUTHOR

Jolynn Freed Regan was born and raised in Fargo, North Dakota. She received her Bachelor of Science degree in Communications with a minor in Creative Writing from Moorhead State University. Regan moved to Malibu in 1998 and immersed herself in the local Malibu poetry scene. Jolynn Freed Regan's work has been featured in *Transformations*, *A Place Like This* and *All Breathing Things* Poetry Anthologies; and in the 2021 and 2023 City of Malibu's Student Poetry Anthologies. Regan has served as a featured reader for the past six years at the City of Malibu's Annual Poetry Summit. She was a featured reader at Malibu's Summer Jubilation Poetry Events in August 2024 and July 2025. Regan is a regular contributor to Malibu's "Verse About Town" program, featuring her poems in public spaces throughout Malibu. She is thrilled to serve the Malibu community and teach poetry at the four Malibu public schools with Ricardo Means Ybarra. Regan has served on Malibu's Poet Laureate Committee since its 2016 inception.

ACKNOWLEDGEMENTS

With deep gratitude to my husband Tim, whose love and support over the past 38 years is boundless; and to my remarkable children, Spencer and Sophie, you never miss a moment to celebrate my poetry and encourage this dream. You are both my heart! To Shandy, your snuggles were invaluable to my creative process. Thank you to my chosen brother, Ricardo Means Ybarra, you have patiently guided me in this Chapbook dream. Your expertise, encouragement and rock star energy are why this book is complete. To Kathy Eldon, my Red Lady Spark, there are not enough ways to say thank you for your commitment to *Just North of Malibu*. To Ann Buxie, thank you for your wise, insightful guidance and stupendous editing skills. I am forever grateful! Huge thanks to art maven Carla Marlenée Bates for your creative explosion of *Just North of Malibu's* front and back cover design. Your vision is impeccable! Finally, to magnificent Mel, much love for sharing your stunning sunset photo for the back cover of my first poetry book. Together with all of you, we did it!

www.ingramcontent.com/pod-product-compliance
Lightning Source LLC
LaVergne TN
LVHW050611100826
845148LV00015B/3225

9798234070425